FOUND

On Bathroom Walls

WILLIAM JAMES LINDBERG

POEMS SELECTED

By Brandon Pitts

COVER PHOTOGRAPHS

Uncle Elizabeth's Internet Cafe

Found on Bathroom Walls

Penhead Press Chapbook Series #3
First Print Book Edition April 2015
ISBN: 978-0-9887938-4-2

This book was formatted, edited, and published by Penhead Press.

PENHEAD PRESS

PO Box 115 · Willamina · Oregon, 97396-0115
www.penhead-press.com

PREVIOUSLY PUBLISHED WORKS:

- An Autumn Walk
  Previously published as "Issue 2 Recap," in Randomly
  Accessed Poetics, No. 3, Sifting Through Raw Words,
  Penhead Press, 6/21/2013

- Anti-Photonic Illumination
  Previously published as "Issue 4 Recap," Randomly
  Accessed Poetics, No. 5, Antiphotonic Illumination,
  Penhead Press, 6/24/2014

- Monsters Have Blue Eyes
  Previously Published as "Issue 3 Recap," in Randomly
  Accessed Poetics, No. 4, Heart Splatters into
  Significance, Penhead Press, 12/21/2013

- Independence Day
  Published by Hoarse, No. 4, End of Summer Field Day,
  University Book Store Press, Seattle, WA, 2012

- Choir Boy Seeks Goth Girl
  Published on Craigslist in the Man Seeking Woman
  section. It ran for several months between 2008 -
  2009. It didn't net any dates.

A Note On Bathroom Walls

What is it about remarks on bathroom walls - you can't not read them. They are not all gems of literature but sometimes, something will stick. Found on Bathroom Walls scribbles its wisdom in our psyche, lets us savor each phrase, each sound created by words found and folded in together on the page. William is a true poet, a person who finds beauty in words others would consider just trash. A teardrop in time turns into a poem about his father, moving home turns into an epic, a whole movie caught in a paragraph.

This volume is the result of many years work by a man who carries a notebook around in his back pocket. He is passionate about the craft and good at it. If you want the full effect, though, read it through with your ears. Read it aloud and listen to the music of the words. He will reach through an unseen realm until he connects his voice to yours. It's a rush, but be warned, he's not afraid to be crude or jarring or to get gritty and raw; it was after all found on a bathroom wall.

Now that you have this volume in your hands, please don't rush, I beg of you. Poems, any poems, but especially these poems are meant to be taken in one at a time. Put this on your bedside table or by your favorite lounge chair and let them come to you one by one. They are the missing link between you and what you forgot, and what you wanted to say. Get drunk on his words, pass out of your mind into his, I guarantee it's worth the trip.

Parting thought, read the table of contents out loud. You might find a collage poem there too.

Carla Blaschka
Author of In the Soup

A Note On Bathroom Walls   7

I: *PAINTED OVER STERILE WALLS*
the World Was Drawn   17
  in Parallelogram Lines
Understanding Somebody, Maybe   18
Worry   19
Blocked Up in Tall Grass   20
Lands End   21
It Is Getting Close to a Year Now   22
Old Yellow Ball   23
Deep Fried Tears   24
Other Possible Realms   25
Laying Down in Bed   26
Love Poem, Attempt 1   27
Maw of Tomorrow   29
Fall Birds   30
Maya in the Garden   31
Where Did I Go   32
Degenerate Art Impressions   33
a 53 Second Haiku   35
It's in the World   36
Crossing the Red Sea   37
a Psychic Reads the Earth   39
The Law is Always Just   40
Life as a Popcorn Salesperson   41
Love Poem, Attempt 2   42
Gypsy   44

The Attraction Was Magnetic   45
Unseen Connective Tissues   46
About Writer's Block   47

II: *WORDS FOUND, EAVESDROPPED, CIRCLED, CLIPPED, OR CROSSED OUT*

These Are My Words Now   51
Paper Sheets   52
Lines Lifted From Books & Conversations   54
Tasting a Lover   55
Are the Gods Good   56
Bitter Medicine   57
Found On Okcupid.com   58
Love Poem, Attempt 3   59
Salty Waters   60
Found On Page 49   61
Pizza Truth   62
a Line From Here & There   63
Driving With the GPS Turned Off   64
Unexpected Journey   65
Explosions in the Sky   66
an Autumn Walk   67
Love Poem, Attempt 4   68
Pandora's Valentine   69
Anti-Photonic Illumination   71
Wildwood Hotel Signs   73
Talk of the Nation   74

French Dip   75
Independence Day   76
Monsters Have Blue Eyes   77

III: *PROMPT WORDS & LINES
      SPLATTERED ACROSS A MIRROR*

Roy Street Coffee   81
Get Hitched or Say Bingo   83
Conclusions   84
"Someday This War is Going to End"   85
Cheese Takeaway   87
a Webcam Free Write   88
Bukowski Wouldn't Like It   90
Titillating Anvil   91
House Across the Alley   92
Love Poem, Attempt 5   93
Feast of Misgiving   95
Triolet for Maximos of Tegucigalpa   97
@Tmacn21, Here's Your Poem   98
Bukowski Hates Form Poetry   100
a Frankensteined Sestina   102
Francis Mount's 6 Word Ride   104
Ben Dover's Smut Palace   105

IV: *READ ABOUT IT ON A STALL*

Love Poem, Attempt 6   109
Sexting For Oedipus On Craigslist   110
Fast Times On Ridgemont Heights   112

Love Poem, Attempt 7   114
Stall Talk   115
What Not to Write in a Love Poem   116
She Looks Lovely Covered in Earth   117
Spam Email Pantoum   118
Love Poem, Attempt 8   119
I am a Bitch   120
Hump On this   121
Pursuing Phony Play   122
Curious Girl Seeks Cougar   123
Did You Happen to See Me   124
Choir-Boy Seeks Goth-Girl   126
I Play Hard but Don't Bruise Easily   128
Love Poem, Attempt 9   129
Poem Unknowingly Read Before a Lady's
Prayer Group at an Open Mic in Everett   130
Washington

About the Author   133
Acknowledgments   134
End Notes: Remembered Sources   135

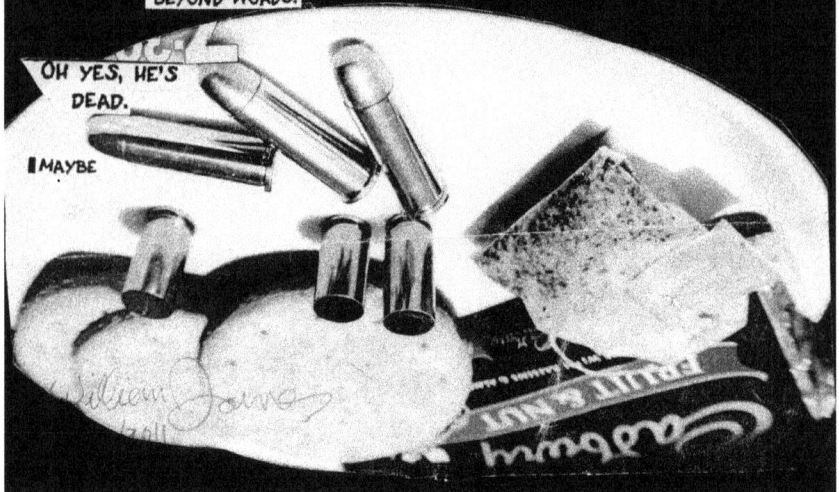

I:

PAINTED OVER STERILE WALLS

THE WORLD WAS DRAWN IN PARALLELOGRAM LINES

It is always wires with mom
She doesn't distinguish between
power supplies
telephone lines
coaxial cables
extension cords
or audio adapters
to her,
they are simply wires

It is true,
some people exist
in different worlds
A multiverse
of crossing lines

UNDERSTANDING SOMEBODY, MAYBE

My father threw a cup
across the room
It narrowly missed my mother
standing ground
by the stove

When I gaze into that window
I see thousands of faces screaming
The sands of reality shift
in the evening breeze
to reveal a mirage

The portal of (my) mind
was fractured
a long ugly scar
broke the window
in the kitchen

WORRY

My mother is ill
She hasn't been able to talk right
for 20 hours
Strained squeaks fill the kitchen
every time she does try
My thoughts drift to...
it's not time yet for that...
eventually, though
all systems wind down
and stop

Small changes become permanent
Her mother woke up with a closed throat
Four days later she passed away
Milo, the dog tap dances across the floor
He can't tell us what he wants

Last night
I dreamed of the Emerald City
I was approaching a steep hill in a car
I was excited
I started to drive up the hill
to see what lay on the other side
It was my last day in the city
This was my last chance

Rain fills the sky
Water seeps up
from the depths of the ground
The atmosphere
is filled with danger

Blocked Up in Tall Grass

It was a cancer
eating the hood of a dodge
that ruined my life

LANDS' END

At lands' end
there exists a spirit
that whistles
un-melodically
through tall firs
and leafy alders
The spirit howls
like a puppy left
too long alone
and you can see it
It rises off the swamp
like evaporation
of morning dew in June
The nearest neighbor said
the day i moved into
the old farm house
that the Farmingtons
covered an ancient
burial ground with swampy water
Under a harvest moon
angry ghosts kill calves and
steal golden grain
off corn stalks in the field

IT IS GETTING CLOSE TO A YEAR NOW

It comes in frantic gulps of air
the realization
my father
is dead

OLD YELLOW BALL

Nails bound
into a board
shimmered
The form began
to take shape
of a knotty pine
coffin

Painful stars
drawn 'cross eyes
filled
with shame
It was a foreign face
A yellow
thorn
burrowed
into the stomach
Its finger
pointed
towards
the liver

A timid
hand
grasped
at the hem
of a skirt

DEEP FRIED TEARS

Garish Orange
and tan lamp shades
illuminated a sign
over a callout
window

Hunched over
people
sat at tables
eating greasy
burgers and limp fries

A cacophony of slot
machines
ground out
a new song
everyone heard
over and over and over

A tired baritone
hailed out the number
Seven - Seven - Zero
from behind a teal screen
adorned in wavy red
yarn

I looked at my receipt

It matched

Jackpot

OTHER POSSIBLE REALMS

She wrapped herself
all around my masculinity

He looked at her
Me
Smirked
Started the car
Told us to get dressed

You remember that man
I talked to
at coffee hour

Well
you don't want to become
like him

He is one
lazy
son of a bitch

LAYING DOWN IN BED

I want
to dream
nice
dreams

flowers that pollute
the sun
breaking my back

LOVE POEM, ATTEMPT 1

It takes hours
buckets of cold Showers
to erase your signature from my mind
I'm in a bind
how do I make this rhyme

The next verse
could be something like this:

Quivers, shivers, fevers..., levers........., beavers

Burning hot
magma
flowing
melting
innards

gizzards ejecting stones bones demonstrative gooey.......
eyed *SOAP*?

NO - NO - NO

that won't work

What is this dribble
that I scribble
to you on the page
beautiful sexy babe

[sigh]

I love that thing you do with your tongue
through my ear tickling my brain
the squishy wetness is kind of queer
when in fact you aren't even here
but talking
miles away
on the
telephone

MAW OF TOMORROW

I don't know what this new sun will bring Brad

I can't read these tea leaves in my cup
They are scatter-shot up to the rim to that place
where hot lips join smooth porcelain

"The future is not the fate we make
the future is the past
the past is now the now
the now just is..." Brad conjectured

I'm living on the ledge smiling into the gaping maw of
tomorrow

I can hear a trickle in the distance

It is dark

I drink

FALL BIRDS

Fall birds speaking chattering tongues
assemble at the train yard
Swirl around billowing like pillars of smoke
after starting one formation then changing their mind
they settled back down between rusty lines of boxcars

Over and over again the flock danced
following one leader then another
darting different directions
gathering momentum for autumn's journey
After the noon sun ascended above the fog
the yard revealed silent cars spackled white

MAYA IN THE GARDEN

It is all in the mind
you know
life
living here
breathing

that wood pecker
beating on a drum
fancydancing
calling out
for a new spring
mate
over yonder

isn't real

this is all a dream

soon
the dreamer
will wake

you
and I
and all that we know
will cease
to be

WHERE DID I GO

Would I miss Mass
if I stopped going
altogether

Today I was scheduled to go into work early
I didn't put up a fuss
What choice did I have

What I question more is
am I still a believer
Does the church teach truth
Is yesterday still relevant

Have I become my father
He worshipped god in nature
at least that is what mom said
I always thought he was an atheist

I, however, experience god
through the scribbles of my pen
and through the croaking
of the frogs under the stars

DEGENERATE ART IMPRESSIONS

A man on a bus
told me about
Little Red Riding Hood
She wore a hooped dress rounder than the moon
She bent down to look between her legs
She observed a boat floating into another world
A toothless man
with dentil probes for fingers
stood knee deep in mud
He wailed on a three stringed harp
he sawed the bloody bow
across a bodice made of rusty nails
he sang, "give it to me now," in a dreary tenor
An old woman
waited for a bus
her back was bent double
from a lifetime of reward-less work
She dragged a mannequin by the hair
It had a twisted face and blue wax skirt
It melted into the moon
as it wiggled and screeched across the sidewalk
Morose dancers
contorted their bodies
as they replayed the scene of the crime
They stirred piss in hell's caldron
with long femur bones
and served the soup
to angels masquerading as reptilian aliens
Lion dogs' screamed murder
they jabbed spears of their rage
between bars of the cage

A deformed man
made love to a machine
he produced children of agony
Bee people boiled out hives
hanging like Christmas tree bulbs
from an ornate cathedral ceiling
They stitched with long finely tuned strands of saliva
melodic shadows of torment
onto primordial cave walls

"High up, there are things waiting to be seen,"
the man at the bus stop said
"I am going"
"soon"

All day
a Cow eats
Grass
Renders
To
IDeas
Rooting
Through
the soil

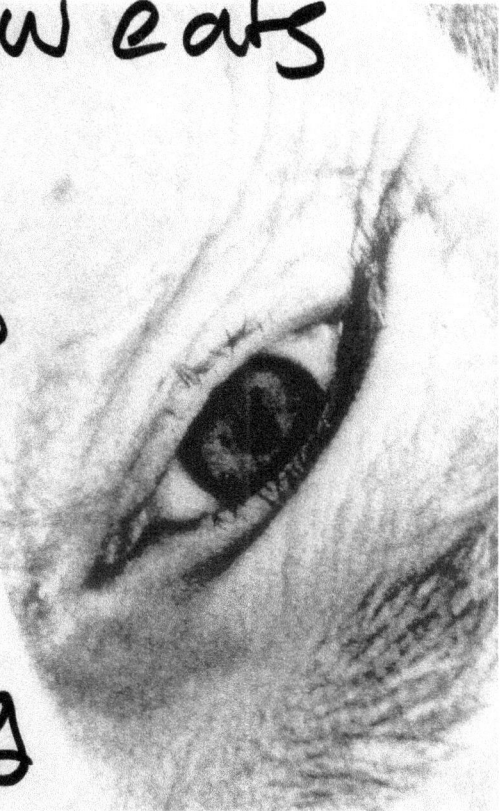

IT'S IN THE WORLD

I had a dream
I saw a fetus with a cold
It was the same color as earthworms
It was in a cage
The floor was dusted by sawdust

A parasite had been released on the earth
It caused madness
before the victim perished
A man shouted
"Hail Ceasar, we who are about to die salute you."
He wore a tall blue hat
His sword turned to water in his hand
He danced with a cheetah
He won the day

Worms crawled over the unborn on the ground
Their unformed noses seeped wet with snot
The queen fly said,
"When the truth is ugly even a lie is beautiful."

CROSSING THE RED SEA

The process of death is the systematic removal of all that you love from your life. It is like taking a prolonged stinging shit. Instead of the toxic byproducts from digested food being eliminated, the essence which animates your soul will run like diarrhea drips out a gaping asshole. Increasingly, as time progresses, your body will become fouled up by experiences unimaginable as a child
The taste of living will be yucky on your tongue. Eventually, even your wobbly steps will become torture and you will begin to lose hope of regeneration. As your last breath nears, a lifetime of anxiety about this day will melt away into anticipation and the finality of escape.

When I moved from the city to the country,

I started to die.

WAR
hammers
eu-phoria
into society
with
KISSING
FISTS

A PSYCHIC READS THE EARTH

Weaved into a pile of oak leaves
a 50-caliber machine gun plays hide-n-seek
mounted on a desert stained Toyota truck

Patriots, rebels, terrorists, or what have you
hoot, holler, spin the turret about
spit fire at this-n-that

She wears a flying bandanna-scarf
red against blue-black
Her face twists into churning contorted emotions

Moldy leaves camouflage against the dirt
raked into a decaying heap near the mulch machine
on the last day of fall

THE LAW IS ALWAYS JUST

This evening on my way home
from Seattle Door & Window, I
tripped over a gigantic pile of horse apples
from a proud downtown mounted cop

That same cop, on First and Union, wrote
a bent old man a ticket
for failing to bag up a steaming pile
of his Cocker Spaniel's crap

Why doesn't the strong arm of the government
have to clean up its own shit

LIFE AS A POPCORN SALESPERSON

I'm trapped in pause
alternate lives streak past me
I want to taste them

LOVE POEM, ATTEMPT 2

The current is swift
The tide is about to shift
I can feel a gentle tug on my waist
It's clear blue 85 degrees out
    (which is hot for Newport in July)
I want to play till dusk in these waves
The coolness of the Pacific lifts my body up and carries me
to the shore

There are dangers here
Yesterday, a shark warning was issued
The day before that a dog was killed by a jellies chasing
a Frisbee into a wave
The ocean is not a tame woman
If I get caught by a rip tide
I could be swept out to sea

The horizon sky looms near
"Red skies in the morning, sailors take warning"
I am the Mediterranean Ocean
She is the Indian Ocean
I've set sail toward Antioch and Byzantium
Her course was set for Mt Olympus
and the mysterious Orient

"Red skies in the evening,"
Wizened sailors sigh and begin revealing
about a point, a mythical transformative spot
where all the oceans
and bodies of water of our world meet
churn together to form one sea

If I stay here much longer
the tide will be going back out
The warning signs have been posted
I am chest high as a big swell approaches
I brace myself against the tug
The current is potent
I laugh in the foam
I am not afraid

GYPSY

She inserted her gaze into mine
I turned the key and locked her in
She stalked to the right
I stepped left
We glided synchronized
like broken hands around the face of a clock
She shimmered
like a windblown blade of grass in the sun
I moved closer
Her apple blossom lips
were animated into a nonverbal conversation
She tightened the circle
I frivolously brushed her arm
She embraced me lock-step into a swing
Her moist flesh quivered under the strength of my hands
I inhaled deeply her natural musky scent
My manhood was instantly inflamed
She pulled me smiling into her loins

THE ATTRACTION WAS MAGNETIC

Mandy loved sexting. She knew that there was something prehistoric about her gender identity. It was like she cast the shadow of a coyote in the evening sun. Coyote would run to the steam to catch fish in its mouth.

Mandy knew there was no such thing as a magical pot of gold at the end of blue-green stripes in the sky.

She frowned when the apple of her eye did not return her affection in a timely manner.

The light was growing dim in the room.

The narrator of the story pulled her off the stage with a long curvy cane.

Unseen Connective Tissues

I feel you
so intensely
I swear
you must

experience
me
as well

Reaching
through
the unseen
realm I

connect
my name
to yours

ABOUT WRITER'S BLOCK

The problem I have had as a writer is that I am blind to the elemental nature of story. I cannot scribble further than my nose. My characters are -plegic deaf-mutes who dialogue gibberish and adventure into a plot of unsold film.

In my day dreams, I compose epic tales. Create archetypal characters who start simple but achieve greatness. Who, with a sword, ray gun, and spell book, save the multiverse from the entropy of nature. However, thus far, I have failed to complete a novel, which is probably why I write poetry.

The words I compose spin round and around a single feeling. I tend to describe it with a wind screaming through a grove of alder trees along the licking shores of a shallow creek.

But ever since I started back at employment, the earth of my mind has emptied itself like the pages filling a blank journal. My book is un-writing itself into a white expanse of hushed chaos.

Well PIMPS

WE'RE ALL PUFFED UP *Now*

Eat

Drink

SMILE *party*

the cows aren't coming home.

WE want to join with you in

The Ocular Concern

ALEXEY KRASAVIN

The Giant

AT THE

END OF
THE WORLD.

II:

WORDS FOUND,
EAVESDROPPED,
CIRCLED, CLIPPED, OR
CROSSED OUT

THESE ARE MY WORDS NOW

my heart swoons
sexy-ugly tweedy
which I oppose
what do they tell
sue me, it's hilarious
undying
guilty American pleasure
or is it
rather
a symptom of the time we live in

like how do I get more than six things in here
including bikes, skis, tent, sleeping bag, camp stove, ...

someone just told me

this sounds

A - D - D

PAPER SHEETS

I hate going to the Doctor
watching agonizingly slow tics of a clock
sitting in endless lines of chairs
surrounded by sick people
coughing
snuffling
hurling
moaning

I waddle through sterile doors
hunched over like a scarecrow
goat in a snow frozen field
Getting on the scale
was like adding insult to injury
The nurse looked at my chart
scribbled a figure
raising a disapproving eyebrow

I was finally led on a leash
to room number sixteen
the exam bed was wrapped in the usual crispy wax paper
I felt like a limp steak
waiting to go into the freezer
I stare at ceiling tiles
reorganize the annoying buzz of lights
into vaguely recognizable patterns
I wait some more
in cubes stacked like Tetris boxes
I cough loudly
I'm still here
I'm still sick
Where are you

The doctor enters after an hour
I vomit out all the sordid details
The doctor smiles nods and scrawls

As a melodramatic whole
the process is far too exaggerated
for a bitter bottle of pills
only the few can afford

LINES LIFTED FROM BOOKS & CONVERSATIONS

I dreamed of worms. They swam under people's skin. The whole world was infected by these worms. When I woke, my heart raced superfast. I thought of it like the human race was walking around the moon with a bone on.

I was having a bad day. I did like the doctor said, I pissed in the car. I tried to put my dreams away into the realm of hobby. I moved from one part of myself to another. The world dissolved around me in a pendantic cloud of versification.

Tasting A Lover

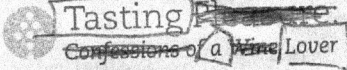

Tasting Pleasure
Confessions of a Wine Lover
Jancis Robinson

In this book, Jancis Robinson traces her love of wine to a dinner date when she was a student at Oxford. Her boyfriend ordered a bottle of a 1959 red Burgundy that was so profound she never stopped thinking about wine. After school, she went to work for a travel agency, and wherever she went, great wine experiences seemed to fall in her lap, eventually landing her a job as a wine journalist for a British publication.

Years later, I saw her speak at IPNC (International Pinot Noir Celebration), and she remarked how she had never really planned anything; that almost every important turn in her professional wine life had been due to external forces pushing her in certain directions. For me, that sense of destiny is the beauty of the wine world. After all, not many people spend their childhoods dreaming of becoming a winemaker or playing "wine retailer" with the neighborhood kids. Almost all of us end up here as the result of those whimsical "external forces."

Source: Oregon Wine Press | April 2013

Her boyfriend
stopped THINKING

When
she went to work
She never planned
anything

Destiny IS the
BEAUTY of
the world
dreaming or

PLAYING

with
neighborhood kids

all of us end up here
as the result of
whimsical external
forces

ARE THE GODS GOOD

To the fat, sign-toting come to Jesus man who played Stairway to Heaven on a clarinet; you're wrong and you look like an idiot. Everything you believe about god is wrong including that ugly ass car you bought.

To that man with the bat on the number 2 bus who tried out a standup routine on us a few weeks before you attacked with an improvised explosive device while shouting, "I have avenged the prophet Mohammed!" You were wearing a wig made of dental floss. Everything got foggy and smelled like ass. You too were wrong for purchasing that ugly car.

Lucky for us all an actual answer came. Behind the text, one can almost hear hardware based music humming, "the gods are good."

BITTER MEDICINE

The doctor told it like it was

Kill the stars
with kaleidoscopic tridents
lest the rays
make prisms

in the deep dark
water
of the abyss

FOUND ON OKCUPID.COM

I'm funny
Like a ninja
in a big bag of awesomesauce
I model green
I hoard music
Dio & Veggies rock
Sushi is rad for fine art nude photography

Heil Hitler
Born this way
is my favorite color
I can't wait to get pregnant
Special happy
Mayo
I am scented

Try to contain yourself
Current pop music is good
Lady Gaga
S&M Rihanna Loud
Fist pumping looks cool
Shocking I'm sure
A real rarity in Seattle

I wonder how long you sat
staring at your computer screen
stressing over every other word
knowing that I am
making fun of you
with my ninja-like reflexes
I love what I'm not thinking about

Love Poem, Attempt 3

We know about the power of

SPACE IN TIME
SMASHING
Your RUBBER SOUL

Those stories you've heard about

THE MYTH of the Impossible

they're true!

—WHO KNEW?

A possible

Mission BEHIND

The Saint and

13 topless dancers

Was

a pregnancy?

59

SALTY WATERS

I heard a feminine whisper
"Is it all right to be here?"

We kissed
Got to the point
I pulled out

The water was black
I could smell
the scent of ivory soap
I heard another whisper
Someone else was in bed beside me
She said,
"is love worth dying for?"

I was not a gentle man
I struck out
with my fist
I felt the sea
pour in
I was drowning

I woke up
Alone
I had, had a sex
dream

FOUND ON PAGE 49

A reason
to live another week

The nightly show
at Broad City

Monkeys
watch
the winter doldrums
under a bus
justified
seeking
women

PIZZA TRUTH

Whatever happened to Donny Strawberry
A chalk sidewalk outline
Is, is not a crime
What does this mean

Cowabunga tank top
Nice legs
Cute butt
Dam, cuss yeah
Boom, boom in de boom box
Sweet moves

Squeeze me
My jeep or yours
New spaces
My juice is sweet like Georgia peaches
I wish I was your lover
You remind me of cool lemonade

Nasty freaky
Alligator inside
Skinny dip
Dance
Summer is here

A LINE FROM HERE & THERE

Have you ever intentionally walked in poop?

Seattle is a city of sun worshippers. Did you notice the man crying? His head faces downward. The sky is murky and purple. It could be worse. I am married now, my sister divorced, my mom sticks her tongue out. We laugh so we may not weep.

My ear plugs fall out in the middle of sleep. We shelter indoors clinging to routine until summer day's return. I felt my nerves burning out of control. It was just like walking in the mud. We didn't tell the others, there was no point. My mother's voice was dramatic and emphatic, with a slightly gruff edge. Where does the universe end and boredom relief begin?

DRIVING WITH THE GPS TURNED OFF

I've fallen in love with a jewel on the waxie moon. She said gimme the loot. I said I know a place beyond the pines. It is mind blowing and heart-stoppingly beautiful. Let's play now in upstream color. Let's be savage and dance naked around a fire. Let's disconnect from the stranger on the television. That alien dictator who drives a little yellow school bus.

UNEXPECTED JOURNEY

When we get older
make new favorite things
Put your pants on
Have an affair
At your desk
In your mind
At work
Mix it up
sprinkle in guilty pleasures
Eat your way into sexy
Remember, she's not your mama
It's play not childbirth
Accept the good feelings
Don't involve your family
Involve your body
Begin living your life
It's not cancer
the end of youth is a new beginning
Explore yourself

EXPLOSIONS IN THE SKY

SEATTLE
AUGUST 2011

cityartsonline.com | City Arts

I was in a bar with some friends

Under the fluorescent lights
, saw-toothed leaves
tickle your cheeks.

The Fringe Pushes In

As you lean headfirst into a dense
tangle of vines
. It's warm and tastes like
sweetness and musk, like summer.
You pop it straight into your
mouth.

AN AUTUMN WALK

I took an autumn walk in my neighborhood. It was the perfect ruse. The comfort of the warm light dimmed as thin clouds crossed the sun's face. I longed to bring someone over here.

I stepped out; put my ear up to the night like a shell. I remembered every neon moment in slow motion. I fell from my mother's arm and slowly poked my way up through brown soil. Her eyebrows said, "Nut Job." I smiled and laughed.

I get fevers late at night, but it's not the DT's. The face of the sun erupted in bleeding arcs of disbelief. I'm no different than I was then. The cement truck made its pour.

Dining at my house was like working off a decadent meal in purgatory. The first thoughts of the statistical brain break upon the quotidian dawn covering all in shades of gray. Her smile tucked like a gun on her face.

Special Moments

Brought Showers
Flowers ... and
Itchy Skin

$2

Tips
on Living

IN

Your CRAP

and Faith

Spring Cleaning the STEAM ROOM

PANDORA'S VALENTINE

I.   Anonymous Entry

Patiently
Attentively
Listen

II.   25% off
Blowing Class

You just couldn't miss
a chance like this
Free first visit
Sleepovers with
theology and psychology
find out where

We won't sell you half a shoe

Condoms reduce the risk

III.   I saw you

Thinking
Big Trouble
Remembering
a Dance
a Game

At some point in our lives
we might as well be naked

IV.

the Reason

SOCIAL JUSTICE

CARE AND

leadership

has ended

W A S

Combat

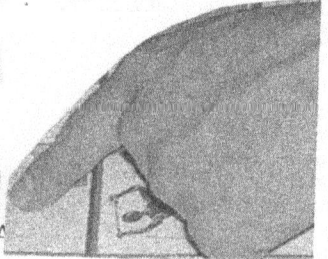

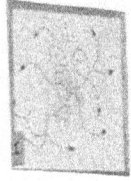

Printed on sustainably sourced paper

LIKE
US

PANDORA &

Jealousy

pushes through
the defense.

14563115

with Little
Sleep

4/30/12

ANTI-PHOTONIC ILLUMINATION

Is this the before
when sin and salvation
hadn't been conceived
and innocent babies wait
their turn to be born
into a purgatory of gloom
where anti-brilliant beings
clothed in blood and flesh
sing without stopping
a din that trumpets through barriers
a runaway train highballs a flash of fire
mapping the path
from flame to pain
in a war of unspoken laws
like Nazis marching on Poland–
where their guns are not as brutal
as the broomsticks they combat
bristles camouflage the phallic end
– longing for a better life
beholden to money and painted women
who carefully arrange love letters and sharp tin cans
in a dead man's shoes
like a blind man identifying a dead child
in a cosmos where
someone is watching
and God
doesn't look like
anyone you know

WILDWOOD SIGNS

The Hill Dogs
Dead End
Killers
Children at play
Be quiet
Stop, look, listen
Blink lights
Injury
Crossing
Railroad
Seeds

TALK OF THE NATION

There was nothing in the investigation to suggest—

His apartment proved interesting
He listened to white metal
Neo-Nazi propaganda plastered the walls
He was kicked out of the army for drunkenness

Almost certainly this man hated Muslims
nevertheless

—he was a monster

FRENCH DIP

They serve breakfast all day

I want my egg eyes up
You're so weird

I got this mental image of you with your finger up your...
You don't pay me attention
You interrupt
You play other roles
I'm just telling
I thought you wanted to go out gambling later
I'm just, I'm..., I'm...
I'm not going bowling with you tomorrow
If you gamble tonight
What's that on TV

....*Your own desire to believe keeps you in that prison....*

You're weird
Not me

[He kisses her]
[She murmurs in clucking coos]
[He cries]

...Do you want soup & salad with that...

Fries

INDEPENDENCE DAY

My brother and I
were raised to be
Republicans

Our mama,
she was a Christian
she centered on gypsy dreams

Our mama wanted the ways of wildness
to wander and to roam

She said,
"That people in America get sick
'cause they live
their lives
in ignorance."

My brother and I were influenced
by the Mormons

We heard men
call young girls
whores
We heard the preachers
who said it was right

My brother and I used to
sneak
into each other's houses
to talk our doubts
and what
we really believed

MONSTERS HAVE BLUE EYES

"Are you okay," he asked

I looked away
haunted
A meaningless count of numbers
jumbled inside my head
If I entomb the memory
under a litany of fractions
sometimes it dulls the pain

A pale sun shines
shuttering the fragment into a moment
Music boiled and foamed
The trailer park reminds me
Faces contort like sun-stained mushrooms

Guilt crests my brow
I imagined callous hands
and the caress of frost clambering between legs
Childlike, not knowing what to do, I collapsed
I spend hours kneeling down on the floor
shuffling through scraps of paper
I uncovered a dozen books on how to breathe

I saw a bird seated on a tree alone
He had blue eyes
9/10, 7/4, 1/3, 1

"There are ways I keep falling,"
I answered, "I am not here..."

TANGO

POT!

PORN

Booze

SMOKE & ICE

SEXIEST SOUNDS

On the Bus with **Electric**

Music

Three Snapshots of THE MULE

Shitting

Chunky Soup

III:

Prompt Words &
Lines Splattered
Across a Mirror

ROY STREET COFFEE

The title was supposed to be clever
"Mr. Happy's Fly Swatter Explains the Status Quo."
The sestina was going to utilize six words
I lifted out of my favorite Big Poppa E poem

The girl, she had a big nose
She was engrossed in a conversation
with a kinky haired guy at the bar
They were drinking red wine
from fat snooty glasses
Coke bottle lenses covered her eyes
Her smiles were magnified across the room
He said that there was no normal
She agreed

I was just standing there, eavesdropping
while I waited for my coffee to finish its drip
I couldn't stand it any longer
I butted in like an orphaned fart in an elevator

I said, I am the icon of normalcy in America
My name is Mr. Happy
I have a fly swatter
I love the sound maggots make
when they swim through a tub of honey
I got a hot water bottle
I screwed the hose
into to a wet-dry vibrator
I found in the laundry room last Sunday
It worked great on Ms. Honey's hole

She liked it more than her cat did
So, I dug a shallow grave
buried the cat
along with the cat food
in the back yard
threw in the flyswatter for good measure
and that empty tub of honey
and smoothed the hole over
with ink that exploded
into my hand from a worthless pen
I purchased
at a super Wal-Mart mega-store

GET HITCHED OR SAY BINGO

A round
burlesque dancer
insolated herself
from reality
inside a lunchbox

She said, "the 'O' was silent panic."

On a webcam
no one can
touch her

She likes it that way

It padded her purse better

"The end result of doing poetry
in April," she said, "was a 40 second
montage on Bill Gates
straddling a vulnerable
nymphomaniac
at a casino bingo bash
expressed
in two volumes of pain."

B4
I (was) sixteen
N33 (said)
G (was) forty-seven
O six-nine

wanted to ~~reach some~~ me conclusions,
so I went to our Flickr pool.

So, yeah, people get ugly when
they're in the grip of joy. We've estab-
lished that. But there's more to it.

I see a photo of ~~Peter Bud~~ per-
forming a dance interpretation of a
Raymond Carver passage, and I can
still feel the awe. I see Macklemore
reciting his eulogy for a friend during
the Poetry and Hip Hop Church, and
I remember the tears I wept. I see an
image of Buffalo Madonna, his face
bloodied during Mad Rad's after-party
performance, and I recall my fear.
And I see a photo of Belle & Sebastian
filling Benaroya's aisles with dancers,
and I swell with joy and think how
very ugly my face must have been.

This festival, which sought to
bring this magazine to life, really
was unlike any other festival I have
ever witnessed. I had spent months
helping to produce something so an
event that would change the city, a
new tradition, but I never expected
that it would change me. It did. I
walked away exhausted, cleansed
and engaged with this city in a way I
have never been before.

Thank you, readers. We'll do it
again ~~next year~~.

Enjoy the issue.

"SOMEDAY THIS WAR IS GOING TO END,"

But not for me
I fight a battle
that will not soon end
if at all
The things I have done
may be forgiven by a god
but not for me

Every day is the same
the bugle
calls the dawn
I crack open my eyes
and the blood of my enemy
has stained my hands
in the night
There is caked mucus
under my nails
I scrub with steel wool
I cannot get clean

In a shattered room
I weep for myself
I see no future
I see only the past
It haunts the rhythm of my heart
Even though I have returned home
to a world of security
I still recount my invasion

Quiet moments scream
bolts of guilt

in thundering storms
I will never be free
till the last breath
escapes
my bluing lips

CHEESE TAKEAWAY

Azalea ran numbers though Katz's device. Pushed the button. The slot machine clanged three times. The jackpot was hers.

Robert was in the playroom. He plugged tokens into the high-stakes claw machine. He maneuvered the appendage over the thousand dollar bill, but grabbed butt plugs instead. Each time he handled a prize, he shouted, "Look folks, another cliché!"

Azalea got careless. She was hauled out of the casino in chains.

Robert wrestled with security. He got a black eye. Later, a sore bottom.

Katz was the big cheese of the operation. His brainiac hacks worked every time.

He kept himself out of danger with cunning schemes.

A WEBCAM FREE WRITE

It would be impossible to describe, in under 20,000 words, how much I don't love you anymore.

The last time we were together was like the first time I went fishing for compliments at a sewage treatment plant.

Your breath stank worse than a plastic door to a latrine in a gold mining town. It was like inserting something into something that should never have had something inserted into it. A dead horse beached on the extra bed for two weeks would have smelled better.

As I walked home that night, I saw your cat lying alongside the road. His legs were frozen mid-stride in a run. It was difficult to tell what was tongue and what was brain's squished out of his mouth. I remember thinking; "my thoughts must have killed it."

I felt bad for your cat too, but I don't feel bad for you. Not anymore anyway. The thing I never understood was why your sister was murdered and what the issue was with the families of the other two victims who woke up in bed wearing the same old clothes.

And when I am phasing in and out of cyberspace, I hope you can hear me softly say, "Save the whales." I hope you listen too, maybe even smile for a change, and walk past that moldy can of spam on the sidewalk instead of picking it up and eating it. Well, you are what you eat though. I just wish you could have moved your feet in a slightly different direction instead sinking in that pit of tar.

Whatever you (don't) do, it shouldn't come as a surprise when the next person—you fuck over—leaves you too.

BUKOWSKI WOULDN'T LIKE IT

The rumors about your potential are true
You could be pure for those who care
Just jump into a puddle of wonderful mysterious chaos

The attendant at Rexall Drugs spoke in shivering whispers
He screamed obscenities behind the darkroom door
He said, "The rumors about your potential are true."

They hang like fortune cookies from bright luminous trees
Braveness is more than the absence of cowardice
     in a fight
Jump into a puddle of wonderful mysterious chaos

or dip a finger into a doubted dark pool of malice
He said, "Iron John is a thirsty fish in a pool of
     holy water."
He said, "The rumors about your potential are true."

Adore the puddle of wonderfulness in your illumination
Compose poems that stick in your mind like wet beer-shits
He jumped into a puddle of wonderful mysterious chaos

He was the main character of your novel
He stepped across a chasm in the twilight dim
The rumors he heard about your potential are true
Just jump into that puddle of wonderful mysterious chaos

TITILLATING ANVIL

Xi's teepee
engulfed
her leaking heart

Her snug
shaper felt like
a paddling
oar

HOUSE ACROSS THE ALLEY

It starts when you are thirteen with an open shade, a pair of binoculars, and a bottle of lube. The woman next door is a looker.

A boy sneaks down the street following a lady. She is young. She meets a strange man in the park. What was that she said. Kissing. It's called French kissing. The man said I went to France once. The lady said then you should know how to do it.

A fly on the wall watches, but this boy listens. Words soak into his soil like fertilizer.

Spying from the closet is not like playing spin the bottle. When there is no warm body in the dark, heaven is long ways away.

You should go she says. I want to paint with you. Let's paint then. She smears red all over his shirt. He paints her hair green. They frolic like fawns in a wood. Her husband looks in the window. Visions of broken bladed glory play on his retinas.

On the nights when she isn't with me I am deformed.

Love Poem, Attempt 5

My favorite places to take girls out are graveyards. Not just any yard, but those soporific lawns where Jimmy Hendrix, Bruce Lee and his son are buried. I also like Goth and Metal; I love how the hyper masculinity and the melodic mournfulness of the attack seep like seminal fluid into my cryptic reality.

Last Saturday, or on that blackened Sabbath day that it didn't rain, a sexy melancholy girl adorned like a night crawler with a pit-bull collar, studded leather harness, chrome chains, brandishing long scarlet nails standing on black nine inch podiums laced to the thigh in scarlet gave me a hand job near a phallic obelisk ménage a trios-ed between the Denny and the Boren family markers. This was as fitting a place as any for a catholic boy who celebrates the death of his savior by planting his seed between fresh cut flowers laid on tombstones to wither into dust.

Jesus was planted in the tomb for three days before he rose out of this womb to new life. This girl she likes the smell of roses. I spray rosewater all over my body and she devours me. Eats my flesh down to the bone, drinks my blood, and uses my ribs to pick gristle out of her teeth. She gets into me like I get into her by way of the throne room where our two beings flow together like muddy puddles of water on a paved side street rippled and spider-webbed throughout by tree roots straining to redefine their space. My fire burns her veil the same way holy water burnt my flesh the first time I touched it to my forehead in Israel. I knelt down in Jesus' tomb and Mary invited me to enter her womb.

I love graveyards. I like to make love on stones saturated with opaque knowledge at that special time of day when the sun bends down to romance the western edge of our world. She is fresh, like a girl flower. I like her scent all over me.

FEAST OF MISGIVING

Fallen leaves smell festive like thanksgiving
Vibrant colors set the table for the coming feast
But for too many, this is only a holiday of misgiving

Little people who've been fractured
    by life's woes and are grieving
Starving for understanding
    it's like their heart has been fleeced
Yet falling leaves still give them festive
    reminders of thanksgiving

Reddish gold's and browns are colors of pleasant endings
They heap up like stars on the ground in the East
But for too many, this is a sign of a holiday misgiving

The greedy few have raised for the many
    the cost of living
Unleashing inside the little people a brutal beast
But when leaves fall people can see the
    approach of thanksgiving

These days are maddening when people are broke
    and no one's forgiving
And it is hard to be giving when love in our world
    appears to have ceased
These realities for many Americans are reminders of a
    holiday misgiving

Thanksgiving is an opportunity to forgive, give
     thanks, and start living
And let our open wounds heal and become like the
     ideal holy priest
Breathe deeply, because fallen leaves still smell
     festive like thanksgiving
But cry a tear for those who are isolated
     in a holiday of misgiving

TRIOLET FOR MAXIMOS OF TEGUCIGALPA

I made the peanut butter sandwiches to the tune of time
Then stole moments to rub a tuna melt on the boss's
    tool-kit lock
Ted, the chef, raised a knife to salute a greasy dime.
He made a million more sandwiches to the tune of time
Ted ground fresh tuna fish into Ponzi-burger
    committing a crime
I vomit out a brain as I work around the clock
Making peanut butter sandwiches to the melody of time
I rob the boss' time to rub a tuna melt into
    a restroom lock

@TMACN21, HERE'S YOUR POEM

I've been kneading
two lines over and over
said to me by a lover
like how a pioneer might,
full of dreams
on the high plains of Pittsburgh
build
out of dirt and straw
a house
This domicile
that should have been our home
realized it was alive
At the same instant
that you departed like sand
through the willow wasp
of an hourglass
Grain by grain
you dribbled out of me
painting movies
of some strangers life
our parents wanted us to lead
on a barrier
locked away
in someone else's mind.
It unfolded
Beating vividly in my chest
throbbing like my thumb did
after I crushed it
with a hammer

when I tried to nail that portrait
of an existence
I never really wanted
onto walls of mud
I rolled up
bloodied sleeves
gritted teeth
blackened by rot
and accepted the pain
clenched between
two intolerant fists
My intellect rejected it
as I flexed the muscle of a brain
given to me by those
who hung pictures
of you in that skeleton
they called a heart

BUKOWSKI HATES FORM POETRY

The euphoria doesn't last long
I squirm around a bit before wiping
I love the feel of cayenne burning in my ass

Wash your hands before touching your eyes
Don't touch your privates either, it can be piping
The euphoria doesn't last long

You might be surprised to know
that cayenne can get your fingers griping
I love the feel of cayenne burning in my ass

You might imagine a dog panting out of control
but will you be able to survive the hyping
The euphoria doesn't last long

Try a pinch or a fistful in your coffee
It will cut through any bad taste such as sniping
I love the feel of cayenne burning in my ass

It's a lot creepier than receiving spankings from a monk
living on top of a mountain sniffing roses and farting
The euphoria doesn't last long
You'll love too the feel of cayenne burning in your ass

A FRANKENSTEINED SESTINA

A red spider
crawled down a filament of cobweb
It was a Frankenstein
a witch
that spun magic in the eve
and cast curses

that really cursed
competing spiders
that crept into the eves
of neighboring houses filled with cobwebs
A good witch
Should be able to tell the difference
    between a Frankenstein

and a Frankenstein
snare woven with curses
brewed by a witch
who can change into a spider
and spin cobwebbing
into all hallows eve

which was this evening.
It was the most magical night Frau Frankenstein
had experienced. She marveled at her cobweb
dripping with cursed
fibers woven by a tiny red spider
a witch

like her could conjure up in the realm witches.
The evening
was waning into a black widow spidery
night only a Frankenstein
in the line of Frau could write into a kissy cursed
sticky fragrant wall of cobweb

No one would want to get caught in cobwebs
scented with the breath of a witch's
curse
The result would be an evening
of torment from Frau Frankenstein's
army of spiders

and her little curses were acrobats swinging
    from cobwebs
only a tiny red spider could navigate. And Frau was
    a witch
one evening a year cobbled together like an
    undead Frankenstein

FRANCIS MOUNT'S 6 WORD RIDE

The joyride was her badge she carried it like rage
on a ruffled polka-dotted clown sleeve
In the hollow of the wilderness, a hidden place of terror,
     Joy found a g-spot

Gee spotted a stain on her sleeve. It became a badge
she wore throughout her life like rage
Hollowed out and wanting, her life wasn't, so to speak,
     a joy ride

Hollow was the rage that drove Joy to ride
her police woman's bike; there was no courage in
     her badge
A mime's sleeve was found in a dumpster soaked
     with Gee's Spot

Cut my sleeve, saw into it like your g-spot, it's not hollow.
Jam it in, twist it around, I want your joy ride
in me like a purple clown's rage rewriting hope
     into my badge

Francis raged into Joy, riding her g-spot
just as Joy demanded till Francis was as hollow
as the badge she wore on a bedraggled clown sleeve

The badge Joy wore was hollow like plastic beads
     sewn on a sleeve
There was no happiness to be found on Gee's spot
When Francis' joy ride concluded all that remained
     was a cave of rage

BEN DOVER'S SMUT PALACE

A rainbow appeared over Smut Palace; the driver of the jet city bus couldn't believe it was a double D. He clipped a tree maiming two kitties engaged in the act of creating something unusual in the dark.

The dark was smothering when Kitty woke in a booth at Ben Dover's Smut Palace. She was confused. Guilt churned the insides of the bus driver as he engaged the machine He had never seen such a dazzling rainbow.

Engaged! It happened on the bus, their trust was sealed by a rainbow. At first she was rattled, but then something enthused in her by the smut Kitty was reading on their new bed. Spinning, she made the room dark.

"Kitty's" she throated, my dark warm place aches. I want your lust to engage magic in my body. I want to gaze into your green eyes ecstatic with rainbows. "Bus six-nine," she whimpered repeatedly, "I knew you; I inhaled your smut."

Bus six-ty was graffitied with a rainbow badly smeared on the back covering a darkly painted advertisement of a dorky Captain Picard fingering the word, "engage." Smut Palace also requested an ad; but the CEO decided instead on yarn & kitties.

Smuttly slathered jam on his toast. He engaged his fingers petting kitties. They purred in delight by his touch. Sensing mice, they darted into the dark. A rainbow appeared over the stop as he waited too long for a number nine bus.

IV:

Read About it on a Stall

(Warning: A few works in the following section could be interpreted as X-rated. If you find
such material offensive, skip back to the beginning or to the very end)

LOVE POEM, ATTEMPT 6

The sea disappears
as her eyes dilate
shimmering reflections
gaze back

moving inside
Logos flees
awakening Enkidu
fingers twined overhead

contorted against the bed
clawing
speaking
forgotten tongues

wrestling as Luna ascends
above the great Earth Mother
Mars, Eros, Agape, Venus fuse into one reality
fires of the deep

pulse and flow
the Un-Named one breathes
new life
into the fertility of her soil

SEXTING FOR OEDIPUS ON CRAIGSLIST

I'll be your female—
your girlfriend
your biological creator
or whoever you want me to be
—in a story rewriting our universe

TOGETHER

Use your fingers
in me
to form words
to show me
how
you plan
to seduce me

BIND ME

into a string of knots
across the page

I want to play with you

USE ME

any way you want

Jack me
Jam me
Poke me
LOVE me

I got a little hole for you to ravish---
it's puckered up doughnut-hole tight
---as long as I can use your member
at the crucial moment
in time

because timing is everything
in this game

WRITE ME

on your phone
when you are at your desk
or at the dinner table
with your wife
or your insignificant other

be my e-male
in an email

only

on the Internet

TONIGHT

FAST TIMES ON RIDGEMONT HEIGHTS

Seeking someone to sit in pj's with all day and play
video games; after we level up, we'll go out and
finish the final treasure hunt together in Seattle
I want someone who can veg out on the couch all night
and still have enough energy the next day to
watch American Idol, drink beer, eat chips, and scratch his
balls

Show me something I haven't seen before
do senseless things run naked
backwards through a corn field
on a warm summer day
skinny dip at the arboretum at dusk
or pluck a banjo wearing an old dress

I'm delightful from all angles
Look at me, I'm in a newspaper
I get excited about ridiculous things
but I draw the line at mayhem
I love all kinds of strength that aren't measured in muscle
I also love short hair, and glasses, and assertive opinions
I'm too conservative to fit into Seattle
but far too liberal to leave---I like Yoga
I am more into plunging directly rather than drifting
exploring the world meeting people
I got my shit together. Do you
By day I live as a web developer
by night you might find me with my arms
wrapped around a guitar or my cats

Promise, you'll like me
befriend me, then seduce me
We all deserve some love action
right, Spicoli

"I don't know..."

LOVE POEM, ATTEMPT 7

Will she groan
out my name
when it is my turn to fill her

I rhythmically ejaculate
A word
with a form that
lacks any
discernible meaning

Through plaster lath walls
The girl next door screams
–Harder, faster, slower

I open my ears
I dream

Alone

STALL TALK

It burns
When I
sit
The pain
in my asshole

This must be love

WHAT NOT TO WRITE IN A LOVE POEM

We're tightly wrapped
our gated breaths overlap
Warm sensations
breed complete relaxation
I am overwhelmed in happiness

A timeless tender kiss
I guard the one in my arms
She, the woman I love
loves me back

Ending never
memories last forever

SHE LOOKS LOVELY COVERED IN EARTH

Does she think of me, O' Swan
The she who wears a myriad of faces
O' Swan, she floats when she walks

Does she get lost in that oblivion of innocence
and youthful learnings
Does she suspect that I have feelings for her
Swan, she enters my dreams and flutters
around like a humming bird
She wears many masks in between her thoughts
Her song bird voice ping-pongs through the space
between my ears

I wish, O' Swan, that you could turn my body's
clock back one decade
But if you did, would I still love her

SPAM EMAIL PANTOUM

Do it with hot looking cutie
Like me; every Single Word
I'm not messing around
Don't bust a nut on a dog

Like me; every Single Word
Get me discretely, at your door
Don't bust a nut on a dog
Are you ready tonight for love

Get me discreetly, at your door
and other women—no strings attached
Are you ready tonight for love
You're invited to play with us

and other women—no strings attached
Use code: SUPER400, hit my slot
You're invited to play with us
First come first serve

Use code: SUPER400, hit my slot
I'm not messing around
First come first serve
Do it with hot looking cutie

LOVE POEM, ATTEMPT 8

I can see her
a seed germinates in rich soil
she is round with my child

I AM A BITCH

A psycho
control freak
I am needy
I have jealous rages
and I want you to be an image of me
but in spite of my flaws
I have an open mind
and want to try something new
My hubby has no idea
He spends too many hours
playing video games
I am losing him
I need a new partner
One with soft curves, boobies, and a vajayjay
I have no idea where this will go
Would you like to hop on a crazy train with me
I am who I am
but I don 't know what I want in a woman
I want to tastes the cakes first
And see where the frosting will take me

HUMP ON THIS

My thighs are as big around as tractor tires
My waist is even larger
I got curves you wouldn't believe existed on Jupiter
It would take a lifetime to explore all the folds in my flesh

But you got to be a big boy to please me
I want a man with a foot long slab of meat
I want a man who knows how to use it as well
Who can control when he comes
And when he comes I want him to come a lot
I want to feel his white hot fury
blasting onto the shield of my cervix
It would be great if you were a multiple shooter too

You don't have to worry about me getting pregnant
because I can't conceive
I was born 47 chromosome XXX
That's an extra X for you to work into my kink
Come on over, big boy, and hump my arm

PURSUING PHONY PLAY

I am a submissive sissy bitch
I want to get you off
Email me your number
I'll give you a ring-a-ling-a-dong

I want to get you off
I can make you feel like a real man
I'll give you a ring-a-ling-a-dong
I want to be cuddled and kissed

I can make you feel like a real man
I am a sweet pretty little girl
I want to be cuddled and kissed
at your place or in your car

I am a sweet pretty little gurrlll
Email me your number
I want to be cuddled and kissed
I am a submissive sissy bitch

Curious Girl Seeks Cougar

I'm looking for a special date
on Valentine's Day
I am a 23 year old girl
seeking an older significant someone
who can teach me a few things

A lot of people say I'm very cute
I'm 5'2 and have long dark brown hair
and I'm pregnant, about 5 months

I can host if needed
but you would have to host most of the time
My boyfriend doesn't know
so, this would have to be a secret
I need to feel a woman's soft touch
I love (the idea of) being with other girls
but don't have to time with my work, school, and gym
to meet anyone to have some nice hot fun with

I'll show you mine if you show me yours...

DID YOU HAPPEN TO SEE ME?

I Saw You

I was the girl with the angry birds t-shirt. You were the girl tussling with crutches. We were on a #4 bus to downtown. I was too shy to talk to you. I handed you a note. In it I said, "*Something precious radiates from your eyes. I feel enthralled to sit in your presence. I am a different kind of person. And I sense that you are too. That we share a kinship in this queer unfamiliar world.*"

I should have gotten over you by now. It was last summer after all that we looked into each other's eyes. When you locked your eyes into mine it connected us to a parallel universe where we could be one body housing two co-mingling souls.

I am lonely without you. Please, if you happen to chance across this ad, write me back my dear sweet (hopefully future) friend. And let us shine our alien lights into this dull world.

CHOIR-BOY SEEKS GOTH-GIRL

for a recurring rendezvous, a blending of opposites:

I'm seeking a cohort to romp through the crème de la crème all the way down into the cracker crust of local metal (or other eclectic) bands; to touch the shape and sound produced by the primal dance of drum and guitar and grinding flesh against steel. I'm seeking a collaborator to pretend to be wealthy, play dress up in fine clothes and share our body heat at a ballroom in a slow winding waltz. I'm seeking a partner to tear it up at a dive bar singing pop or country karaoke. I'm seeking an affiliate to squander our rapidly waning dollar on the latest bilge Hollywood produces. I'm seeking an associate to watch amateur leagues play ball at the park or join in on a Tuesday or Friday night dodge ball game. I'm seeking a companion to break bread–share a meal–discuss politics, films, poets, authors, oddities, art, music, the decline of our civilization, work, spirituality, anything–I can cook. I'm seeking an equal to simply share subtleties rambling through neighborhoods breathing in the ectoplasm of life as it is lived or not.

I'm searching for a lissom energy signature I encountered vibrating through the seat of my soul before the turn of the wheel. I'm searching for somebody, I call "Black Nails," the image of her hand appeared on that veil, which hangs between the unconscious and conscious mind. I know this all sounds crazy, to think that an a-priori connection could occur linking two strangers through that esoteric aether existing between here and there, you and me.

Perhaps we've already chanced 'cross one another: at the Harvard grocery, or Vivace's, or strolling down Broadway, or at the Sureshot Cafe Sunday afternoon's listening to potluck musicians spill fire out their guts, or on a bus, or at a metro stop in the morning waiting and not wanting to go to work-me trying not to drink you in, nevertheless intrigued by the sway of your gait and flit of your hair across your forehead.

Maybe you've seen me and I haven't you near the lake or at a park. A man sitting on a bench with a book or notepad frenetically scribbling delicious lines of verse or humming morose Hank Williams melodies or composing passionate lyrics that somehow appear to fall down from the heavens. Perhaps in your imagination you've encountered echoes of his pounding heart in thunderous applauds of silence-breathing in the now.

Two souls meet, melt into one, a kaleidoscope of mind segmented into body, blended into opposing forces of light dark, yin yang, me you.

Are you her?
        That star crossed lover I visit in shadow of moonlight sonnets splayed 'cross the sky in mysterious swaths of passion: AN OPEN DOOR, A FREE SPIRIT, ELFIN, EARTHY, BOTTOMLESS EYES, LONG WHITE FINGERS–NAILS PAINTED BLACK....

I Play Hard but Don't Bruise Easily

I can't stop thinking about some sexy chick
climbing up and grinding down on my face
like it was her first time driving stick

I have a fantasy...
I have always wanted an enema
I think it would feel soooo nice having water squirted
up my ass then push it out all over your body
Then you can eat me out and fuck me
I have all kinds of toys
Then I would rub your clit and finger you

I am real and have no disease
Just be yourself and we'll get along great

I don't want my face all over the place
Msg me with your picture and number
and I will call or text you

LOVE POEM, ATTEMPT 9

Dutch Masters
eat out
come
give head

rise, sip
stay
rock hard
on top

POEM UNKNOWINGLY READ BEFORE A LADY'S PRAYER GROUP AT AN OPEN MIC IN EVERETT WASHINGTON

Fuck, fuck, fuck, ah yes, fuck
Long division and fucking
Danny Boy's good at only two things
Danny Boy's good at dividing them nuts

Long division and fucking
Lilly Long's there sucking that dong
Danny Boy's good at dividing them nuts
Larry, where's your hut

Lilly Long's there sucking that dong
Your long ass balls are hanging
Larry, where's your hut
Long balls, Larry long balls, yes

Your long ass balls are hanging
Your balls are banging and clanging
Long balls, Larry long balls, yes
Danny Boy's there dividing them butts

Your balls are banging and clanging
Danny Boy's good at only two things
Danny Boy's there dividing them butts
Fuck, fuck, fuck, ah yes, fuck

I stand on the cliff
looking down into the abyss
I can avoid jumping

that horrible place—
—is released

The worst part is that

the anger

will destroy me,

my relationship

sickens me.
have I   fallen?
—Anonymous

ABOUT THE AUTHOR

William James Lindberg is more of a word musician than a page poet. The experience of words oscillating through his bones is the kindling that feeds the blazing frenzy of his pen. He learned the meaning of the word, poet by living on Capitol Hill in Seattle from 2003 to 2011. There he performed poetry at nearly every venue in the city. He also busked his word for a stint on street corners at Seattle's famous Pike Place Market.

William believes that writing is best produced in community with others. He team-taught a workshop (Verbal Expression Lab in 2011) with Ahmed Teleb at Seattle Central Community College, coordinated a writers' circle (2010 - 2011), co-organized a critique group with Carrie Albert (2006 - 2011), emceed a spoken word open mic in McMinnville & Newberg, and produced a cable access TV show that featured writers & artists (2001 - 2003).

William currently lives a Henry David Thoreau fantasy in rural Grand Ronde, Oregon. In the solitude of a hidden valley he gardens words, publishes a zine called Randomly Accessed Poetics, publishes a chapbook series, and tends his websites rapoetics.com & penhead-press.com.

ACKNOWLEDGMENTS

Special thanks to my writer friends: Brandon Pitts, (author of Pressure To Sing, The Annotated Lot, & other works), Duane Kirby Jensen (artist, writer, & curator of Everett Poetry Night), Spirit Ariela, Ahmed Teleb, Brad Walker (mentioned in Maw of Tomorrow), Purple Mark (for taking over leadership and organization of the writing circle), and my family for encouraging me to continue on.

I also thank Carrie Albert, Larry Crist (author of Undertow Overtures), Aaron Dietz (author of Super, In Case I Die, and other books) Priya Keefe, and Charles Leggett who were members of my old critique group, red pen. They played an important role in the formation of my writers' voice.

I especially wanted to thank Carla Blaschka (author of In The Soup) for her role in the creation of this book. Since September 2011, when I moved from Seattle to Willamina, Oregon, she has been faithfully sending me The Stranger every month. She also wrote this book's preface.

Lastly, I wanted to thank Kirk Erickson for providing financial support to penhead-press.com and for pushing me to produce work throughout the past 20 years that I have been pursuing the craft of writing.

END NOTES: REMEMBERED SOURCES

Degenerate Art Impressions was composed at a penhead writing field trip (organized by me and attended by Priya Keefe, Ronnie Porter, Larry Crist, and someone else) to the Frye Museum (Seattle WA) during the Degenerate Art Exhibit (March 19 - June 19, 2011).

Photograph, Uncle Elizabeth's Internet Café bathroom, page 38; the haiku on the mirror was inspired by a line in the film *Imitation Game*.

These Are My Words Now and *Found on Okcupid.com* – words and line fragments were sampled off a dozen profiles found on okqupid.com in 2010.

Ocular Concern (page 48) and *Love Poem, Attempt 3* – were clipped from a fall 2011 edition of Willamette Weekly, a cheesy birthday card (no. 13394113 American Greetings Cleveland, OH 44144), and a pullout ad found in some 2011 edition of the Catholic Sentinel.

Tasting a Lover – Oregon Wine Press, April 2013.

Are the Gods Good – The Stranger, Vol. 24, No. 24, 2/11/2015.

Salty Waters was composed from a few random words and sentence fragments found while reading the novel Salt Water (Charles Simmons, Chronicle Books LLC, 2012).

Found On Page 49 – words & line fragments were sampled from The Stranger, Vol. 24, No. 20, February 2015, Page 49.

Pizza Truth – words were found chalked on the ground at Cal Anderson Park in May of 2010.

A Line from Here and There – You've Been eaten By A Hamburger Zine, Volume 2, December 2012

Driving with the GPS Turned Off – words, lines, and fragments came from The Stranger, Vol. 22, No 32. April 10-16, 2013. Pages 60-61.

Explosions in the Sky – clipped from City Arts, Seattle, WA, August 2011.

an Autumn Walk – see Randomly Accessed Poetics, No. 3, Sifting Through Raw Words, 2012, for line by line bibliographic details.

Love Poem, Attempt 4 – sourced from some 2012 edition of The Stranger.

Pandora's Valentine – was clipped from a cheesy Valentine's Day card (no. 14563115 American Greetings Cleveland, OH), Catholic Sentinel, and the Stranger, 2012.

Anti-Photonic Illumination – see Randomly Accessed Poetics, No.5, Anti-Photonic Illumination, June 2013, for line by line bibliographic details.

Wildwood Hotel Signs is an arrangement of a few choice road and other signs decorating the walls of the Wildwood, a restaurant in Willamina, OR. [The Wildwood Café makes the best French fries in northwestern Oregon!]

Talk of the Nation – ideas were sourced from some radio program on NPR.

French Dip – is based on interesting lines I overheard (or thought I heard) and wrote down at Coyote Joe's (a restaurant) in Willamina, OR in 2013.

Monsters Have Blue Eyes – see Randomly Accessed Poetics, No. 4, Heart Splatters into Significance, 2012, for line by line bibliographic details.

The cut up poem on page 78 was clipped from an April 2014 D-List Magazine and from some 12/2014 and spring 2015 edition of the Stranger.

Someday This War Is Going To End was inspired by a line from the movie Apocalypse Now and some TV news program (maybe 60 minutes) on Gulf War vets suffering from PTSD.

Titillating Anvil – words came from a scrabble game played in 2013.

Feast of Misgiving – prompt line (Fallen leaves smell festive like thanksgiving) provided by Purple Mark Wirth.

Triolet for Maximos of Tegucigalpa – prompt lines (Making peanut butter/tuna sandwiches to the tune of time and Taking time to rub the tuna on the lock) provided by Don Comfort.

@Tmacn21, Here's Your Poem – prompt lines (roll up your tolerant sleeves And.....show your intellectual fists .....flex the muscles of your mind, and give it all to those who have hung pictures of you on the walls of the hearts.....) provided by Tera McIntosh.

Francis Mount's 6 Word Ride – prompt words (joyride, badge, rage, sleeve, hollow, and g-spot) were provided by Kirk Erickson.

Ben Dover's Smut Palace – prompt words (rainbow, smut, bus, kitties, engage, and dark) were provided by Ben Sonnenberg.

Page 106 bathroom wall photograph – Powell's Books on Hawthorne, Portland, Oregon, 2010.

Sexting For Oedipus on Craigslist, I Am a Bitch, Hump On This, Curious Girl Seeks a Cougar, I Play Hard but Don't Bruise Easily, Love Poem, Attempt 9, and Did You Happen to See Me – were either directly sampled or inspired from Craigslist miscellaneous romance, casual encounter, and missed connection personal ads.

Fast Times On Rigemont Heights – The Stranger, Love Lab personal ads, volume unknown, 2013.

Spam Email Pantoum and *Pursuing Phony Play* – word and line fragments were assembled from webcam stripper emails found in a junk folder.

Poem Unknowingly Read Before a Lady's Prayer Group at an Open Mic in Everett, WA – based on a Twitter tweet from @PartyJak, "You got long ass balls Larry, long balls Larry," July 2011.

Untitled Erasure Poem on page 132 – I, Anonymous (At the Edge), the Stranger, volume unknown, published 4/20/2011.

Found on Page 46 (an erasure poem back cover) – City Arts, Visions by Riz Rollings, issue unknown, July 2011, page 46.

www.ingramcontent.com/pod-product-compliance
Lightning Source LLC
Chambersburg PA
CBHW060805050426
42449CB00008B/1547